MANAGING PE

FOR THE FIRST

Ronald Bracey

60 Minutes Success Skills Series

Copyright © David Grant Publishing Limited 1998

First published 1998 by
David Grant Publishing Limited
80 Ridgeway, Pembury, Kent TN2 4EZ United Kingdom

99 98 10 9 8 7 6 5 4 3 2 1

60 Minutes Success Skills Series is an imprint of
David Grant Publishing Limited

British Library Cataloguing in Publication Data
A CIP record for this book is available from the British Library

ISBN 1-901306-08-9

Cover design: Steve Haynes
Text design: Graham Rich
Production Editor: Paul Stringer

Typeset in Futura by Archetype IT Ltd,
Cheltenham UK and Camplong d'Aude, France
http://www.archetype-it.com

Printed and bound in Great Britain by
T.J. International, Padstow, Cornwall

This book is printed on acid-free paper

CONTENTS

ABOUT *MANAGING PEOPLE FOR THE FIRST TIME*

Can you really learn about the basic management skills quickly and easily in just one hour? The answer is a resounding "Yes". This book provides you with a managerial blueprint which will mean your first experience of being in charge will be rewarding, profitable . . . and fun!

How to use this book

The message in the 60 Minutes Success Skills Series is "it's OK to skim". Each book is written in a way that allows you to flick through and find the help you most need.

Managing People For The First Time is a collection of hands on tips that will help you become a really effective manager. It is a guide to dip into for ideas and help. You do not have to read it all at one go or do everything we advise straight away.

Divided into five chapters, this book deals with all the key issues that face everyone starting off in management. Take 60 minutes to find out how to make more use of your management skills and what you need to develop these skills to the optimum. This book will help you to move in the right direction from day one.

You will find that there are some graphic features used throughout the book.

These mean: "Something to think about" – they set the scene and identify the problem areas by prompting you to think about situations which will instantly feel familiar.

With the problems diagnosed, these features give you ideas for an action plan – they will help you to change your behaviour patterns in a positive way.

These features appear at the end of each chapter. They are checklists which summarise all the advice given throughout the chapter. Similar features also appear within chapters which are overflowing with tips!

As you read through the book, you will come across lots of tips and practical advice on how to make a big impact in your new management role. You could start by just going straight to any of the boxed features, which will ask you either to think about a problem or to do something about it and give you some ideas.

If you're really pushed for time, you can always go direct to the tips at the end of each chapter. The chapter tips summaries are also useful reminder of what's where when you come back to look at this book in the future.

Good luck!

What's in this chapter for you

> *What is your management task?*
> *Management styles*
> *The power of thinking*
> *Understanding the politics*
> *Understanding the culture – get acclimatised*
> *The foundations of a brilliant management career*

> ❝ *But be not afraid of greatness; some men are born great, some achieve greatness, and some have greatness thrust upon them.* ❞
> **– William Shakespeare, *Twelfth Night***

If you have just got that career break which takes you into a managerial role, you are about to enter one of the most interesting, challenging and rewarding areas of work – the management of people. You are probably feeling a mixture of exhilaration, worry, intrepidation and panic. This book will help you to channel your positive energy into succeeding.

People management is an imprecise science, simply because human beings have such complex characters. People behave inconsistently and unpredictably, they will change their personalities when in groups and they are motivated by myriad different things. This book will help you to come to grips with managing such complexity. Let's start at the beginning.

What is your management task?

> ❝ *On my first day in a supervisory role I felt a mixture of dread and excitement. I had wanted this chance for ages and when it came I realised that I didn't really know where to start! For the first few months I stumbled around trying to make some sense of it all and learn what was expected of me. Now I'm part of a growing business and feel that I am really contributing to its success. If you asked me to define management today, I'd simply say that it is about making the business successful through getting the best from the people around you.* ❞
> **– Anita Motson, operations manager**

Management has been defined, explained, explored and dissected in many different ways. Thousands of hefty tomes are dedicated to defining what it's all about. Forget all of the theory — what you need at this stage, embarking on the exciting and hazardous journey of people management, are techniques so that you can quickly become effective and make your mark.

Faced with your first management role, your success is going to be measured against how well you can get along with and motivate those around you. It will be a theme that is repeated throughout this book.

Keep the following definition with you all of the time: "Good management is about developing and supporting the environment for success." That, quite literally, is all the pure theory you will have to endure in this book!

As a manager, you will be expected to deliver on whatever key targets have been set for you. These could relate to sales target, building a team, an efficiency saving or penetration of a given market segment. Whatever it is, you need to know and you need to know the minute your management career starts.

Can you define what is expected of you from day one? You cannot possibly be expected to succeed if you do not understand precisely what your role is.

      && *The first three months were really very awkward between my boss and me. I thought that my principal role was to turn the home sales team round. It turned out that the board was more interested in the export potential for the new product lines. This only came out at my first appraisal.* **&&**
– Jane Richards, sales director

Establish what your priorities are as soon as possible.

    ❑ *Get clear guidelines based on your job description or letter of appointment. You cannot succeed if you don't know what criteria you will be judged against.*

❑ *Think how these priorities relate to the members of your staff. Remember, as a manager your job is to get the best out of your colleagues.*

Management styles

Coming up to your first management position, what do you think is your management style?

Do you consider yourself to be democratic or authoritarian, hands on or hands off? What other adjectives would you add to describe yourself? Windswept and interesting, perhaps?

Similarly, you could ask yourself how your birth sign, your relationship with your mother, or your interest in embroidery affects your personality at work. When seeing yourself in a management role, avoid the temptation to place yourself in a neat and tidy box. Life is not this simple!

You can only be a successful or an unsuccessful manager. Don't try to be someone you are not. You have been employed because of who you are – don't adopt a different personality!

The truth is that we all present ourselves to different people in different situations in different ways. A brutal and bullying general manager may send his dear grey-haired old mother chocolates and flowers weekly. A shy and retiring accountant may become demonic behind the wheel of a car. Consequently, you have to be comfortable with your own personality and your own mood swings. Don't be tempted to straitjacket your personality!

"Styles" of management always have their associated problems. A team may not pull together if the manager is seen to be too tyrannical. Managing using negative and controlling behaviour will always cause difficulties. You must learn to adapt your approach to match the circumstances you encounter. Be flexible and respond to each situation as it arises – avoid stereotyping your own behaviour.

Do you recognise any of the following traits in yourself?

- ❑ *I feel responsible for how everyone else behaves.*
- ❑ *I expect people to get the message straight away.*
- ❑ *I wish things were like they were in the good old days.*
- ❑ *I have to spend all of my time criticising and worrying.*
- ❑ *I'm always chasing missed deadlines and feeling savaged by time.*

Be aware that by allowing yourself to be dominated by any of these attitudes you can detrimentally affect your efficiency as a manager.

Consciously try to clear your mind of emotional baggage and commit yourself to responding appropriately to every situation as it arises. Be natural and objective.

There is no single style of management that is successful – all sorts of people, from all sorts of backgrounds make it into the management stratosphere. However, two themes are vital:

○ *the way you think about your role and*
○ *the way you interact with other people.*

Successful people have developed a mastery of interpersonal skills, and few have done so by being aggressive or bullying.

Effective managers understand and accept that people make the difference. Success can be boiled down to having the right people in the right job at the right time. Part of being a management high-flyer is to make the right kind of decisions around the people who work for you. Having a really good people-centred approach is the key to making it in management.

Assess yourself. Are you good at:

❏ *Being yourself rather than playing a role at work?*   Y/N
❏ *Leaving your personal problems behind as soon as you walk through the office door?*   Y/N
❏ *Being true to your own moral codes and values?*   Y/N
❏ *Treating others in a way that you'd like to be treated yourself?*   Y/N
❏ *Balancing the needs of the organisation against the specific needs of individuals that you manage?*   Y/N

If you have answered "yes" to everything on this checklist, brilliant, you probably have a well-balanced approach to life (or a fantastic capacity for self-delusion). If you have two or more noes, you may need to rethink your approach to the management role.

The shifting picture of the "ideal style"

The perception of what makes up a successful management style is changing constantly. The ruthlessness portrayed in the movie *Wall Street*, with the message "victory at any cost", summed up much of the 1980s' thinking. This has given way to a much more human approach. Really successful managers are now more likely to be wearing casual clothes and to portray a relaxed and caring approach to life.

> ❝ *After I'd been offered the position of production manager I read Sun Tsu's 'The Art of War' and some other kick-ass management books. The team I inherited had a reputation for slick professionalism but a degree of eccentricity. I went in, all guns blazing, and took over. Result: eight resignations in the first six months, and a department which barely functioned thanks to in-fighting and low morale.* ❞
> **– Peter Kidby, production manager**

Your new job is about nurturing the talents of those around you and applying those talents to generate creative solutions. You are not being employed to terrify your staff!

Think of someone you know and admire who holds a successful management position. What qualities do they actually have? How much of the image that they portray really contributes to their personal effectiveness?

❝ Once I finally realised that my adopted style didn't suit anybody, let alone myself, I sought help from a consultant friend of mine. He taught me to stop thinking in stereotypes and to believe in myself. The staff responded to the real me almost immediately and a successful new team developed not long after! ❞
– Peter Kidby, production director

The importance of knowing yourself

Self-knowledge and analysis is vital to you as you start on the managerial ladder. You've got to be confident and self-assured and to know your own mind. To achieve this it is helpful to identify your weak points so you can work on them.

Be honest with yourself. Do you:

❑ *always seek a seal of approval for decisions that you intuitively know are right?*
❑ *live in the past and fail to learn from mistakes?*
❑ *do things by the book, even if it doesn't work?*
❑ *see the solutions to problems but lack the courage and stamina to stand by your convictions and persuade others that you have the answers?*

None of these failings is fatal. If you recognise the symptoms you can overcome the problems. You should aspire to becoming comfortable with yourself, willing to take risks and live with mistakes, and forgiving but assertive. Effective managers can:

○ *shrug off difficulties, seeing them as positive learning experiences;*
○ *smile when things go well and boost the confidence of others;*
○ *feel pleased when someone else is successful and show it.*

As a new manager, it really doesn't matter if you are an extrovert or introvert, the life and soul of the party or quiet and reflective. You have been promoted for who you are and the skills you have. What you need is to be confident enough to communicate and develop your ideas and work constructively with the people in your team. This can be simplified if you develop the power of positive thinking.

The power of positive thinking

Is the way you think important? Of course it is. "Survival of the fittest" now hinges on effective thinking skills rather than the physical power of muscle and sinew.

> **❝** *My biggest mistake when I was first promoted was to take with me loads of preconceptions – managers looked and behaved in a certain way, my boss was to be treated with kid gloves etc. etc. Within a couple of weeks, I'd loused up a really big deal because I was scared to act on some information that came from my staff. I pretended I already knew it and didn't want my boss to know that the opportunity had come from one of my subordinates. I left it too late and lost the chance. I realised that I was shackled by my preconceived ideas. I had to learn pretty quickly to think positively on my feet and respond naturally. I feel I have mastered the art of positive thinking and am a much more effective manager because of it."*
> **– Paul Thorson, financial analyst**

From an early age we learn a whole set of rules, beliefs and attitudes through which we make sense of what goes on around us. We carry around "mindsets" – patterns of habitual ways of thinking that we apply to the situations we find ourselves in. Sometimes, these mindsets can get in the way of skilful problem-solving, in which case they can best be described as self-limiting beliefs.

Mindsets are not necessarily bad things. "I believe in truth and fairness" may be an attitude drummed into you by your parents from an early age, and to be governed by such beliefs would be considered a "good thing" by most people. However, telling yourself "I've never been good at talking in front of an audience" or "I'll never understand basic business finance" can mentally block you from developing new skills and talents.

> Try to identify the negative mindsets that are holding you back. Never say "I can't do that." Think, "I've not been able to do that it in the past, but I'll learn how to now." Confront your weaknesses head-on and they will gradually disappear.

> ❝ *I was twenty-one when I was put in charge of my first shop. I'd been brought in over a couple of more experienced people and they were ready to trip me up. The first week was fine until my day off – I'd gone home with all of the keys! They couldn't open up or take any money until I arrived shaking with rage and embarrassment. I never fully recovered from that and it wasn't until I moved to a new company that I regained my confidence.* ❞
> **– Phill Crane, retail manager**

You will make mistakes. Everybody does and sometimes they can be horribly embarrassing and make you look a complete idiot as in Phil's case. However, you do have a choice when disaster strikes. You can pack up and spend the rest of the week in the pub, wallowing in self-pity. Or, somewhat more constructively, you could stand tall, admit you fouled up, apologise to anyone badly affected by your mistake and, if possible, laugh!
When you make a mistake, there will nearly always be benefits.

> Aspire to perfection . . . but don't be a slave to it. Profiting from errors is the part of the learning process.

You can change the way things are done and ensure that you are more in control in the future.

Don't get too engrossed in worrying about the future. Put it into perspective – what is the worse thing that can happen? Usually the things that have kept us awake at night, panicking, turn out to be not so bad after all.

To put your worries into perspective, try keeping a diary for a few months. Write in it the forthcoming issues that are troubling you. Review these once they have been resolved. Invariably you will find that the outcome you feared wasn't so terrible after all and that you coped. Don't waste time worrying when you could be planning for your success!

Another element of positive thinking is to avoid jumping to conclusions. From day one in your new position, always try to test out or to confirm any opinions you arrive at. You may sometimes get the wrong end of the stick – with potentially disastrous results. Similarly, you may be deliberately misinformed.

> **❝** *I was really flattered when my opposite number in the sales department took me for lunch and told me she was there to help and how much she was looking forward to working closely together. I fell for it! I immediately concluded she was a true team player. It turns out she was angling for the departments to be merged, with her at the head, and all she was doing was ripping my ideas off and presenting them as hers. I was so naive!* **❞**
> **– Angela Parker, marketing co-ordinator**

Don't start from the premise that everyone is out to stab you in the back but, at the same time, be a little reserved, even suspicious, during the early stages of your new management position. Get to know the personalities and the internal politics before trusting anyone totally.

Understanding the politics

> **❝** *Three days into the new job, I couldn't believe what I'd landed myself in. It turns out that my boss was running a personal war of attrition against the rest of the company. As his right-hand man, I was seen as a major threat to all those around me. If I'd had an inkling of what the situation was at the start, I could have prepared myself a great deal better.* **❞**
> **– Chris Noakes, sales manager**

Any organisation is built on a whole host of collective and shared perspectives. To align yourself successfully and quickly you need to get into this culture and to develop the art of understanding the rules and expectations.

Some organisations seem to be dominated by politics. As a new manager, the games that people will play to stay one step ahead or to push colleagues down may well appear to be baffling and a terrible waste of energy. However, if you do not follow the rules and understand the dynamics it could well be that the politics will destroy you.

Tips for coping with the politics

❑ *Observe, absorb and keep out of it for the first few months.*
❑ *Align yourself with your boss (unless he's obviously on the way out himself!).*
❑ *Go to the right meetings and get involved wherever possible in key decisions.*
❑ *Make it clear to your team that they have a job of work to do and that you do not want to be managing a department of Machiavellis.*
❑ *Don't align yourself with individuals until the whole picture is clear – they may have ulterior motives!*
❑ *Don't get too involved with personalities – remember the corporate good.*

> ❝ *I'd only been with the company for a few weeks when I discovered that the new finance director was planning on doing away with about half the current team. I got caught up with the politics and set up to champion the cause of those people who were favourites to lose their positions. The boss took me to one side. She explained that a financial crisis was threatening the whole organisation and that those people earmarked to go were largely the ones responsible for the mess. I avoided one of the biggest mistakes of my life. Nowadays, I never act without considering the big picture.* ❞
> **– Liz Crowfield, management accountant**

Another dangerous aspect of politics is failing to see the "big picture". Without the big picture decisions may seem to be perverse when in fact they are brilliantly well executed and timed to perfection. Often people collectively fail to appreciate the fuller picture so they reflect on their immediate personal short-term, knee-jerk perceptions. Seek out the big picture. Understand the strategic framework that your organisation is operating within.

More on winning at the politics, or at least not getting damaged by them, will be learnt in later chapters when we look at how to handle meetings and corporate communication in general.

Understanding the culture – get acclimatised

There may be a huge set of "social rules" that you'll need to observe to be accepted as part of the company. There may be 7.00 a.m. breakfast starts or regular social evenings out and you may need to conform.

So, how can you be sure that certain aspects of corporate life are truly important?

Are you aware of the history of your organisation and department? Seek out colleagues who have a long-term perspective and get a potted history (together with the myths and legends) as to why things are done in the way they are. Has anybody tried to change cultural aspects in the past and, if so, are they still key players?

Some of the culture may be ritualised and outdated – designated parking spaces, executive washrooms etc. etc. This is often characteristic of companies that have stagnated, or family businesses where it remains terribly important for individuals to massage their self-images.

If you find yourself in such an organisation, ignore or scoff at your peril. You may be able to contribute to changing things but you will only be able to do so over a reasonable period of time.

As a general rule it's best to be non-judgemental, certainly at the beginning. As the "new kid" you don't want to get a reputation for being difficult when you have only just started. Other people may spread around your negative feelings quite happily and use them to undermine you.

Seek out your organisation's mission and vision statements. These may be hidden in company reports or they may be emblazoned across publicity information or on an internet web site. Check out your understanding with other people and try to get the balanced view of what your organisation is really about.

Think of the detail. Is there a dress code? There will be something of a herd instinct that you need to comply with – at least until you get accepted. Challenge these traditions at your peril.

Very few large organisations continue for very long in their original form and function. Every walk of life is undergoing rapid development, with the pace of change tied to technology and information. To help manage this process you have to be one step ahead, the theme of chapter 2.

The foundations of a brilliant management career

If you can develop the right fundamental attitude to management from day one, you'll be unstoppable!

Work on emulating the qualities of successful managers.

1. In reality you can't *learn* to be a particular sort of manager. You are not Marlon Brando, immersing yourself in the role and method acting your way into management. Be yourself. People will see through a charade.

2. Assess your strengths and weaknesses to identify the areas you'll have to work on. If you treat people with respect they will be far more forgiving of your shortcomings.

3. Learn the power of positive thought. You will have good days and bad days and things will not always go right for you, but to be successful you should learn from such experiences. Avoid using self-pitying statements like "things never go right for me" or "I'm always fouling up". With the right "I can do it" mental attitude you can do, can risk, can recover and can change.

4. As you move into a new management position it is essential to know precisely what will be expected of you. Clarify any grey areas before you start. How can you shine if you don't know all of the criteria you will be judged on?

5. Don't jump to conclusions. Be cautious about aligning yourself with particular people and ideas. Get an idea of the "big picture" – remember, you have been employed to serve the whole company, not to collect hobbyhorses which lead the business nowhere.

6. As a new manager you will be expected to fall in with the prevailing culture. Even if you are passionately opposed to some of the cultural quirks, you should not tackle them head on – wait until you have become accepted and then use gentle persuasion and reasoned argument to bring about change.

What's in this chapter for you

Understanding the basics
Your value to the organisation
Reporting
Getting to know your staff
The first big meeting
Learning from your boss
Crimes and misdemeanours
Get off to a flying start

❝ *On the first day I sat in my office not knowing what to do. My boss was continually in meetings, nobody phoned and nobody came in – it was as if I was invisible! When the same thing happened next day I decided to introduce myself and get involved. By the end of the first week I'd managed to identify the key people and begin to understand the basics of what I'd been employed to do!"*
– Geoff Archer, design studio manager

Understanding the basics

In your new role you may be able to hit the ground running or you may be faced with a steep learning curve. It will probably depend on whether you have been promoted internally or are joining a new company.

If you are in the latter situation, a good organisation should provide you with some kind of induction course. If they don't, then ask for one. It doesn't have to be terribly formal or structured. Even being walked round the company meeting people for a couple of hours is extremely useful. This will help you to get some feel for your role and the people that you will be working with.

❝ *My self-organised walkabout was vital but it didn't give me the full story. It was quite a while later before I discovered why there was aspirin dispenser in my office!* ❞
– Geoff Archer

Regardless of what's formally on offer in terms of an induction course, you need to gain some insight into the organisation at various different levels. Ask questions at the earliest possible stage – preferably before you even accept the job.

○ *What is expected of you as an employee?*
○ *How long is the post expected to last, if appropriate?*
○ *How does the position fit in to the rest of the organisation?*
○ *Why has the job become vacant?*
○ *What happened to your predecessor?*

Within the first week of your new job make sure that you find out:

❏ *Who the key people are – their roles and your relationship to them;*
❏ *How departments and individuals interact;*
❏ *Which key meetings you have to attend;*
❏ *The key processes and how things get done in the organisation;*
❏ *How much responsibility you have.*

Make sure you're clear about these factors before your honeymoon period is up. Of course, there will be routine administrative tasks that you will have to understand fully, relationships to build and develop, strategies to follow, but you will learn and do all this as you mature in the job. However, you need to understand the basics early on.

Your value to the organisation

Most importantly you need to be aware of what difference your job really makes to the organisation. This may sound fairly obvious but you are only valuable when you are genuinely adding value. Think of the Pareto Effect or the 80/20 rule. Around 20 per cent of a company's or a person's activity accounts for 80 per cent of the business success. Get this 20 per cent well identified in your own position and you'll know from day one where to concentrate your efforts.

❝ *Working with Geoff was very frustrating indeed. Creatively, he was brilliant, but he always did things at his own pace and would constantly sidetrack himself into irrelevancies. Consequently, he*

was never promoted and in the end left through frustration. If he'd only known when to prioritise and how to get himself noticed, he could have really gone places. **99**
– Barry Wollocombe, advertising director

You can build up your knowledge of the organisation and your role in it logically. There may be an organisational chart to consult. Use it to locate your own position within the overall context of the organisation. Identify the areas which are the major cash generators, or which add most to the overheads, and how your responsibilities relate to them.

Reporting

You also need to establish what is expected of you in terms of formal and informal communication. Some companies (and some bosses) will require a four page memo from you every time you visit the toilet. Others try to cut formal communications down to an absolute minimum. If you can learn and supply what's necessary at an early stage, you'll have a better chance of hitting the ground running.

Before undertaking any task clarify the following:

- *Is a formal report needed, or a memo, or will a verbal round-up suffice?*
- *Who should be copied in?*
- *If a formal response is required, will you need to do a formal presentation and, if so, to whom?*

If the culture that you have come in to is very heavily based on formal reporting, you need to comply with this, at least in the early stages. However, you can get yourself noticed and make yourself very popular if you add pithy summaries to such reports. That way, you are complying and giving people what they expect, but you are also offering them the opportunity to absorb your message quickly.

66 *My predecessor would take the reps' weekly reports and produce a regular monthly update on the state of the market. This often stretched to 30 pages, which I suspected nobody could find time to read. I kept the tradition going for the first few months but added a synopsis of the key points. I then asked for some feedback on the*

value of the report and was pleased to have it confirmed that people were only reading the summary so I stopped producing the full version. 🗝
– Martin Adams, regional sales manager

In the early days, do what is expected of you in the manner expected, but look for ways to add value and to get yourself noticed. Being innovative, flexible and delivering on the key issues will certainly help you to make your mark quickly. Remember: people will welcome a change if you show them that they will benefit from it.

Getting to know your staff

Increasingly, work is based around teams of people who are encouraged essentially to manage themselves. A common primary management role is to lead these teams.

You need to make an early impact on your team. You can do this by spending some time getting to know them and asking them for feedback on their roles and how they see the team progressing. It's often a good idea to talk to them first on an individual basis, allocating ten minutes per person for a brief informal "getting to know you" meeting. These can be followed up with an inaugural team meeting, for which you should schedule at least one hour. Ideally this process should be completed within your first week. This way, you are all together straight away and you should be able pick up the dynamics of the team.

Tips for running you first team meeting

❑ *Make it appear to be relaxed and low key so that everyone feels comfortable.*
❑ *Have your own agenda, preferably written down, but try to allow the meeting to run as spontaneously as possible.*
❑ *Plan the environment in which you are holding the meeting. It should be distraction-free and you should ensure all calls are diverted.*
❑ *Make an introduction, saying a little about your background (if you are new to the company and if you have not*

> *previously done so) and stressing your belief in the need for teamwork in forging a successful operation.*
> - ❏ *Encourage feedback. If people are reluctant to speak initially, pick out the most confident looking members and direct open questions at them such as "How do you feel about . . .?"*
> - ❏ *Don't let anyone hijack the meeting. If they do, interrupt by saying something such as "Let's see what the others think" and direct a question to someone else.*
> - ❏ *If the team has had problems and morale is low, don't ignore this fact but also don't allow the meeting to turn into a mass moaning session. Stress that you and they must look forward and that you are committed to work with them to ensure future success.*
> - ❏ *If they are not so already, make such team meetings regular events – weekly if possible.*
> - ❏ *If an important point of procedure is raised, minute it. If it involves a change in working or policy and you are unsure if you can agree it then clarify the position with your boss and report back your findings at the next meetings.*

Remember: if you commit to given action, make sure that you do it! Nothing will undermine your role more than being seen not to deliver on points agreed in the meetings.

Leap-frog syndrome

Whether you have been promoted from outside the company or internally, the chances are you will have leap-frogged over someone on your team who had expected to get your job – rightly or wrongly they are probably feeling overlooked and undervalued. This person may be someone who consciously or unconsciously holds a deep resentment towards you.

> ❝ *I found out pretty quickly that I'd beaten an internal applicant for my new job – and not in a way that did anything for my reputation! The person in question deliberately implemented one of my suggestions, even though she knew I'd make a mistake. It caused a major setback and it wasn't until the embarrassing post-mortem with my boss that I discovered I had a major hostility problem to deal with.* ❞
> **– Johnny Osmond, systems manager**

The first thing to do is to find out if this is indeed the situation. You should do this by asking your boss or the personnel department directly about the background. Once you have identified a potential problem, you need to sit back for the first couple of days at least to see how, or indeed if, the difficulty will manifest itself.

Look out for the following signs:

○ *Attempts to undermine your authority – this may show itself by way of acerbic comments in the office or on the shop floor, or a confrontational attitude in meetings.*
○ *Aggressive/resentful body language.*
○ *Unwillingness to co-operate – they do as you ask of them but slowly and with poor grace.*
○ *Downright refusal to do as you ask.*

What would you do in such circumstances?

What to do to combat resentful staff

❑ *Firstly, establish that the problems are genuine and not the result of NBP (new boss paranoia).*
❑ *If necessary, ask your boss or a trusted colleague to verify your impression.*
❑ *Confront the individual as soon as you're sure a problem exists – if you ignore their behaviour, your authority will disappear, not just with the problem person but also with the rest of the team (and your defeat will be talked about with relish by the victor!).*
❑ *Explain that you know the situation and understand how disappointed they are. However, make it very clear that you believe you are the right person for the job.*
❑ *Ask for their support and help as a valued member of the team, and if possible entrust them with some extra quasi-managerial tasks.*
❑ *Attempt in the first instance to win them over without compromising in any way your managerial authority.*

Try **all** of these tactics, as to do otherwise may appear vindictive or cowardly to the rest of your team. But what do you do, if after several weeks of understanding behaviour from you, you still feel that they are pulling against you and disrupting the team?

Management is about compassion, but it is also about taking tough decisions. Ultimately, if someone is refusing to respond to you, then formal disciplinary action has to be taken, in full consultation with your boss. The end result of this may well be that you have to fire someone for the first time. Are you prepared for this?

The first big meeting

By now you have made your mark as a leader and have an understanding of how to achieve your goals within the framework of the organisation as a whole! The next likely hurdle is your first management meeting, when you'll be in full view of your bosses and your peers. This is your golden opportunity to make a positive impact!

> ❝ The company had a full-blown management meeting at the end of my first week. I was very nervous about it but also aware that I needed to make an impression on my boss and the other managers. I made sure I read all of the recent minutes of previous meetings, and made a list of points to make. Some were just to seek clarification on things I didn't understand; others were serious suggestions about future strategy. I know the meeting went really well and that I had made a big impact because the MD suggested I should join their strategy "think tank", which I have since learnt is a rare privilege indeed! ❞
> **– Jane Newman, editorial services manager**

You need to understand the role and function of the meeting and you can do that by reading the minutes of previous meetings. Look for key themes and "saga" items – those which come around time after time. Try to clarify the following issues:

○ *Do you get a sense of order and direction or are the minutes all over the place?*
○ *Is there an action column? And do people get taken to task for not delivering on a project?*
○ *Is everyone expected to contribute?*

Do some detective work. Ask people about the rules of the meeting. Is it formal and do you need to talk through the chairperson? Do you need to take turns on questions? Precisely who will be there that you need to impress?

So you are well prepared for the first management meeting. What are the golden rules you should follow?

Coping with the first big meeting

❏ *Make sure you are punctual. Allow yourself plenty of time if you have to travel to it.*
❏ *Make sure people know who you are! You will probably be introduced to those around the table, but if you are not then introduce yourself at the earliest possible opportunity (but don't interrupt the MD or CEO to do so!).*
❏ *Ask pertinent questions. If you don't understand an issue or a procedural point, ask an intelligent question. Avoid speaking just for the sake of it.*
❏ *If you have a valid contribution to make then do so. You want people to sit up and take notice.*
❏ *Avoid expressions such as "In my last company we used to do . . .". Use questions such as "Has . . . ever been tried in this case?", which are forward looking and challenging.*
❏ *Even if the meeting is the most boring event you have ever attended (with the possible exception of a Phil Collins concert), don't show it. Yawning, looking at your watch, scratching your head (or anything worse) and staring out of the window will immediately make you stand out as an outsider.*

Meetings take up endless hours and cost companies millions of pounds annually. However, they are a necessary fact of company life and to begin with you have to put up with them and shut up. When you are more experienced in management and more secure in your position then read in detail more about how to make meetings effective. At this stage, play the game.

Learning from your boss

> ❝ *I made the mistake of bursting out laughing when my new boss was describing his pet project. It seemed to me as crazy as trying to sell address books to hermits. He didn't appreciate it and began to marginalise me. My position quickly became untenable.* ❞
> **– Richard Wright, unemployed**

Your boss should be your best role model at this stage – let's be honest, he or she appointed you so you need to prove their decision right! Understanding their role and what makes them tick is important. They may be in charge of many different departments of which yours is just one and so you need to see their relationship with you in its full context.

Without embarking on a PhD in sycophancy, you should also identify key pet areas and what the boss considers important. You may well think these things are nothing short of petty, but punctuality, accuracy, hitting deadlines, reliability, even the clothes you wear can damage your relationship irreparably early on.

Be up front and explain that you want to learn as much as you can. Most bosses will be flattered (you're not a threat) and will generally be pleased to help.

If you suspect that there is a problem and that perhaps the boss feels threatened by you (you're younger, better qualified, more outward going, and a better golfer), be sensitive to this. Ask lots of questions and seek their advice to reassure them that you fully understand the hierarchy and who precisely is in charge.

Crimes and misdemeanours

Seeing the world from your boss's perspective will help to enhance your relationship and your own personal effectiveness. However, don't follow everything blindly to the letter. You have been added to the organisation to help it work more efficiently. The key is to address the shortcomings in a positive way and avoid causing any offence. To do this requires mutual respect and the easiest way to engender such a relationship is stay in your boss's good books.

Be wary of the following misdemeanours and, as far as humanly possible, avoid committing any such "crimes":

○ **Not delivering**
Don't assume that your boss will forget about that report you promised would be finished in three weeks' time. If you have a real problem with it (e.g. you don't understand the issues, haven't got the time or the resources) come clean as soon as possible. Help may well be offered from a source you hadn't previously considered.

○ **Blame shifting**
If Lorraine in accounts hasn't delivered the costings for your report, it's down to you. Blame shifting comes across as weak and ineffectual.

○ **Worshipping Janus** (the two-headed god)
Moaning in the bar about your job, the boss, the company or the people you manage can backfire. Your sincerity and commitment must never be compromised by careless talk.

○ **The "not in my job description" mantra**
You should assume that your job is elastic and that in the early stages you are there to please. (However there must be limits to your beneficence – if you find out the cleaning contractor has been sacked and the vacuum cleaner, mop and bucket have been deposited in your office, you can safely assume you are being taken somewhat for granted). Use your common sense as to what is or is not reasonable.

○ **Assuming that the company revolves around you**
Your contribution may be very important but you have to appreciate the big picture. As a general rule, if you're only in charge of 10 per cent of your boss's total area of responsibility, you will only warrant 10 per cent of your boss's available time.

Get off to a flying start

Mapping out the critical success factors will be the key to you delivering results as soon as you hit the ground.

With a comprehensive plan of action, you can start to make an impact from day one

1.   You should already have a clear understanding of what is expected of you and have gained some ideas about the organisation as a whole from your induction. Use this to build a picture of where you fit in and, more

importantly, which parts of your role generate most value for the company – it's in those areas where you should focus your efforts.

2. Investigate the reporting processes and make sure you can supply the necessary information to the right people right from the start. Find out who is there to help you in this task.

3. Get to know your team straight away. Begin with short informal individual interviews and follow up with a full team meeting, preferably within your first week in the job. Institute regular full team meetings if they don't already happen and make sure you take action on the things you agree to.

4. Invest some time in getting a sense of how the organisation works: e.g. relationships with customers – what is the interface? How do the finance systems work? What are the production processes used? Where is the value added to products or services?

5. Seek out role models who do reflect the corporate ideal and possible mentors – these may be people who are spoken about a great deal or individuals who are doing similar jobs. Use them for their specialist knowledge, their contacts and their impartiality.

6. Learn about your boss's beliefs and values and emulate them as far as appropriate. You will not be able to sway him or her if you don't develop a mutual respect and this will not happen if you begin criticising right from the start.

7. Don't be afraid to propose changes if they are needed but do so only if the timing is right and your argument shows that the company as a whole will benefit.

8. Prepare carefully for your first big management meeting by reading the minutes of previous meetings and making a note of the key issues. This is your chance to make a mark with your peers and superiors.

9. Concentrate on not committing any misdemeanours which will undermine your reputation – e.g. don't be tempted to shift blame wherever you can, own up quickly if you realise you are going to miss a deadline, and never adopt the "it's not my job" approach unless it really, really isn't.

What's in this chapter for you?

Forging a winning team
Making people hungry for success
Reining in zealots; encouraging laggards
Leading from the front
Managing former colleagues
Managing people older than yourself
Dealing with difficult people
People principles

Forging a winning team

The late Matt Busby, manager of Manchester United Football Club, often suggested to superstar player George Best that he needn't bother to turn up for team briefings. As he explained, the advice he gave to the other team players was to pass the ball to George as quickly as possible!

There are very few organisations where the single contribution of one individual can make such a tremendous difference to success. Most businesses are dependent on the collaborative working of thousands of employees. Your success now depends on you being able to lead your team effectively.

> ❝ *We had hit a creative block on one of our key projects and were discussing the problem in the weekly team meeting. Jill, our team administrator, who had been as quiet as a mouse since the time she joined us, broke the deadlock with "Why don't we . . .?". The effect was startling – all of a sudden we were having an incredible brain-storming session, which gave us not only the basic idea but also the means to make it work. Until then, I'd never really appreciated the collective strength of my staff.* ❞
> **– Robert Solomon, team leader**

A team is basically a group of people with different skills and competencies who by working in unison are able to achieve more than when working in isolation. They are consolidated by sharing the rewards of their success. Some tasks can only be achieved through teamwork.

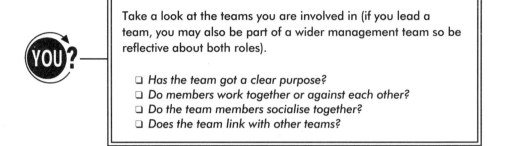

Take a look at the teams you are involved in (if you lead a team, you may also be part of a wider management team so be reflective about both roles).

❏ *Has the team got a clear purpose?*
❏ *Do members work together or against each other?*
❏ *Do the team members socialise together?*
❏ *Does the team link with other teams?*

Teams only work effectively if everyone has a clear understanding of what their role and aims are. If you doubt that this is case within the team you are leading, you need to find out why, and do so quickly.

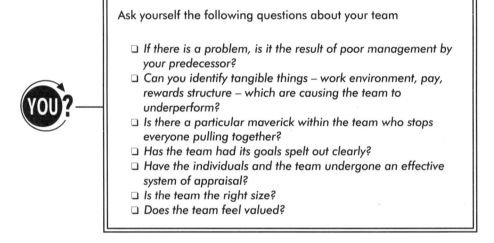

Ask yourself the following questions about your team

❏ *If there is a problem, is it the result of poor management by your predecessor?*
❏ *Can you identify tangible things – work environment, pay, rewards structure – which are causing the team to underperform?*
❏ *Is there a particular maverick within the team who stops everyone pulling together?*
❏ *Has the team had its goals spelt out clearly?*
❏ *Have the individuals and the team undergone an effective system of appraisal?*
❏ *Is the team the right size?*
❏ *Does the team feel valued?*

By understanding the dynamics of the team, you will get a sense of where to take it next. Much of this can be learnt at the regular team meetings discussed in the last chapter.

Let's look at some ways to tackle the most common problems encountered when taking over a team:

○ **Poor management in the past**
   Enthuse them, ask for their, meet with them, cajole them, excite them, challenge them – anything to get them to sit up and take notice and realise that you are there to change things for the better.

○ **Malignant maverick**
Decide quickly whether the individual is simply a misunderstood genius or a genuine pain in the neck. If the former, you want them on your side so consult with them and ensure they feel valued. If the latter, you may well have to get tough and formal if their performance and behaviour does not improve quickly – the team's morale will suffer if you do not act rapidly.

○ **Garbled goals**
Discuss continuously with the team what their purpose is. If necessary, write it in big letters and stick it to the wall where they can see it every day. Make all your judgements as to how both the individuals and the team as a whole perform against these overall goals.

○ **Ineffective appraisal**
The company you are in will probably have an appraisal process which is undertaken once or twice a year. Make sure you use the system enthusiastically and understand all of the processes, but in addition make sure you are appraising and evaluating the team and the individuals constantly on an on-going, informal basis.

○ **Wrong size**
Is the team too big to act as a cohesive whole? If so, then think of ways of breaking it down into "pods" – inter-pod competition if . handled sensibly can be a great motivational force.

○ **Low self-value**
There may be resentment about remuneration or working conditions. You will need to look at each individual case and, if you feel justified, argue for improvements. However, be careful not simply to agree with everything that is being asked of you just to make everyone think you are a wonderful person. Never allow yourself to be manipulated – always take an impartial view of the situation.

❝ *I was in a fantastic self-managed team. We could decide how to do things, how much to pay ourselves and it really worked well. However, a new guy who just wasn't into being flexible joined us. We'd stay late to sort out a problem while he'd leave bang on time. We confronted the situation and he moved on – he said that he wasn't a team player. The trouble is that there is a shrinking market for lone wolves.* ❞
– Terry Jones, engineer

Your role in the team is critical as you don't want to dissipate or lose any creative energies. You also need to balance the development of the team against the development of the individuals.

The characteristics of a good team – open communication, challenge, delivering on projects – can be easily measured.

Most of us like to have a sense of purpose, success and reward. Being part of a team can provide for all of these important psychological needs. It can be the most satisfying way of working, if the right conditions for development and growth are in place.

Invest time getting your team feeling comfortable. Set aside regular periods for everyone in the team to participate in "loosening up". This form of team building, which is very often best undertaken away from the work environment, can cover a variety of activities. It could involve fairly conventional pursuits, such as a night out ten pin bowling, playing darts or pool, or an established course offered by outside consultants.

If these sorts of activities are already going on when you join, you should encourage them and throw yourself fully into the spirit. However, if they are not and you have no budget for such things, then do not push for them in the early stages. It may be that they do not fit with the current company culture.

Teams need to work together with a measure of mutual respect and trust and this will take time to build and to maintain. However, consider implementing quickly at least some of the following ideas to ensure that you make a big impact on all the members of the team:

○ *Brain-storming sessions*
Encourage free thinking on given problem areas. When someone comes up with a solution pass it on to the next member to develop. You will find this gets people interested and amused, and you can end up with some brilliant ideas.

○ *Allow the team to make its own rules*
If the team members are going to be truly committed to the corporate good then empower them to decide how this is going to be done. Of course, you will face some flippancy (e.g. let's double our salaries, work half the hours and have a fully stocked drinks cabinet) but this will help to relax everyone so treat it light-heartedly. You will find that the team take their power seriously.

○ *Encourage early discussion of problems*
If something is troubling either individuals or the team as a whole, you need to hear about it fast to stop trouble escalating

○ **Introduce a suggestions box**
Encourage ideas and innovations – offer monthly prizes for the best ideas.
○ **Encourage honesty and openness**
If someone has a problem with another team member, then this should be dealt with directly and honestly between the two. Similarly, back biting and gossiping about other members should be completely banned.

Consider a team charter incorporating at least some of the above which clearly states how team members are meant to act towards each other. Everyone should agree it and sign it and the charter can then be displayed prominently for everyone to see.

Making people hungry for success

As a new manager, you may well be taking on individuals or whole teams of people who feel demotivated and undervalued.

> ❝ When I took over the department, morale was seriously low and I was told in no uncertain terms that they were all going to leave unless serious money was put on the table. I agreed with them that there was cause for complaint in terms of their salary, but I also explained clearly that with the present budgetary constraints, an en masse pay rise was impossible. I then looked at how they worked, how they viewed themselves, and spent the next year really working on motivating them. It worked – no one has left and they are a great team!❞
> **– Karen Masters, hospital administrator**

What sort of incentives can you use to move individuals or the team forward?

Money is a big motivator for obvious reasons. However, it is unlikely that you will be able to drastically increase everyone's salary immediately, even if you feel that such action would be justified. Further, people work for reasons other than the purely financial benefits.

When you want to increase people's motivation, consider the following:

○ **Skill levels**
How well trained are the individuals? Would they benefit from specific training courses to help them learn new skills or new technologies?

○ **Recognition**
How much feedback do they get? Does anyone bother to say "thank you" or "well done"? Start doing so immediately – recognise excellent work formally with a brief congratulatory memo, copied to your boss if you feel that would be appropriate.

○ **Money**
Is pay a problem? If you believe that inequities exist, then commit to levelling them out over a given period of time. If increases themselves would be impossible to implement, can a bonus scheme or performance-related pay be introduced?

○ **Environment**
Are conditions fair? Is the work environment contributing to or detracting from success? Can superficial changes – positioning of desks, flexible working hours, drinks/break facilities – be improved?

Leading from the front

❝ *It was quite a shock when I realised that people saw me as their leader. I suddenly found people wanting to check out the most trivial of things with me. They saw me as some kind of commanding officer who would shout at them if they got it wrong."*
– Lousie Dixon, healthcare manager

What makes a good leader? Can leadership be learnt?

To get individuals or a team working to their full capacity effective leadership is essential. As a new manager, it is unlikely that you will stride into your office on day one and captivate everyone with your Churchillian leadership qualities. Leadership is something which develops with experience over time. However, the following tips will help you to begin the process of becoming an effective leader.

How to develop the skills of leadership

- ❏ **Get Organised!** *Ensure that you are on top of paperwork, that you deliver on time and that you plan sufficiently in advance. You may consider seat of the pants management to be Bohemian and endearing. Your staff will simply view you as having no control over them or yourself.*
- ❏ **Learn to Communicate** *Write and speak clearly and ensure that what you are saying is understood. If you are in doubt, keep checking. Think in terms not just of what you are saying but also how you are saying it. Think too of your non-verbal communication skills – eye contact, posture, how you dress and how you use personal space.*
- ❏ **Be Assertive** *It's something of a cliché to say "be assertive, not aggressive" but it is true. Stand up for what you believe in coolly and calmly and do not allow yourself to be bullied by others.*
- ❏ **Be Consistent** *People need to know precisely where they stand with you so ensure that any of the criteria that you have set, against which you will be judging success, do not change. Do not move the goal posts!*

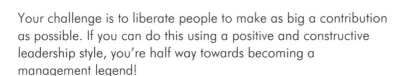

Your challenge is to liberate people to make as big a contribution as possible. If you can do this using a positive and constructive leadership style, you're half way towards becoming a management legend!

Managing former colleagues

Having to manage people who may have recently been friends and contemporaries can be fraught with problems.

> ❝ *I'd joined the organisation straight from school and gradually been working my way up. I was a young man with no responsibilities and used to enjoy socialising – going to the pub, having a laugh. When I was put in charge of the lettings staff, I knew quickly that I had to change. I was still approachable, but I knew that I could not still be one of the gang in the evening and manage the team effectively the next day. It took some of the staff a while to recognise the change but for most of them the transition was seamless.* ❞
> **– Adrian Porter, senior housing officer**

In truth, if you know what your role is and behave in an appropriate manner, then the team will quickly accept the new status quo in most cases. People will be pleased that you have been successful and, if you are following the advice in this book, will be delighted that you are there to make them successful too. However, the chances are that, to begin with, you may well experience some difficulty.

If you have just been promoted, think about the existing relationship you have with the people you will now be in charge of. Can you foresee any problems? For instance, will you have trouble if you need to discipline the self-appointed team prankster and motor-mouth who you used to spar with?

People may expect old friendships to transcend the new relationship. The best way to knock that on the head is to dazzle them with new ideas and practices – you've changed and so will they!

If someone persists in refusing to accept you in the new role, then you have little choice but to confront them. Explain that you understand the difficulties change can bring but that they have to be working with you for the long-term benefit of the team.

As for Adrian above, should he stop socialising with the team now he is the manager? Of course not! He should still go to the pub with his team (even suggest it himself), but he should avoid over-indulgence or any compromising behaviour which will diminish his standing.

Managing people older than yourself

This is more likely to be your problem than theirs. We tend to associate age with concepts like respect and deference. We also tend to associate older people with individuals who have had some control over us in the past such as parents, teachers and our first bosses. This can make you feel uncomfortable when faced with managing people old enough to be your parents.

❝ *George was 59 when I became department head and I was more than a little unsure how to handle him. I became even more worried when I saw him making the sign of the cross before he switched his computer on! I soon discovered he was a complete gem. His experience is beyond value – I've lost count of the number of problems we've solved thanks to a few words from George. He's taught me, and the others in the team, endless tricks of the trade – not a professionally jealous bone in his body, and a true gentleman. I wouldn't be without him!* **99**

– Paul Springer, production manager

As with managing former colleagues, the truth is that most people will accept being managed by people younger than themselves, assuming of course that you treat them with the same respect as you give to the rest of your team. The world is changing and older people are used to seeing success come to others at a very early age. Also technology is moving at a baffling rate for some people and that can be viewed very much as a young person's territory.

Avoid the temptation to think that because you've made it and they haven't, you are a superior being and that they should be packed off to pick up their pension. Perhaps they never felt inclined to climb the slippery pole of management and they are totally happy with their lot.

> You'd never dream of discriminating against someone on the grounds of their sex, religion or colour, would you? So, don't be ageist!

Remember, too, older members of staff with a long service record can give you excellent insight into how the company is run – use their knowledge whenever you can.

Dealing with difficult people

Often we have to make compromises. For instance, there could be some people in the team we'd rather not have around. There may be a longer term game plan but in the short term it may be necessary to make a pact with the devil.

66 *Better to have him inside the tent pissing out than outside the tent pissing in."*

– Lyndon Baines Johnson, poet

Solutions to difficult people can be managed as part of your medium-term management strategy.

❍ *Make it clear to everyone that the team is only as good as the weakest link.*
❍ *Also, spell out your expectations of other people's performance.*
❍ *Be prepared to offer support and guidance. Also, be forgiving . . . but only up to a point.*
❍ *Always operate within the boundaries of employment law.*
❍ *Be honourable and you will only attract respect. Be too ruthless and you run the risk of becoming stuck on your own sword.*

Regardless of age or status, you will inevitably at some time have to manage people who seem to thrive on being awkward and difficult. When (note, *not* if) you do, try out the following approaches.

With difficult characters . . .

❏ *Find out if they have a particular problem (at home, perhaps, or with a workmate, or with you) and see if you can identify a possible solution.*
❏ *Be direct – if they are upsetting you and the rest of the team, tell them. Get things out in the open.*
❏ *If they are really trying to provoke you, don't rise to the bait. If you lose your temper, you lose your dignity. If the situation reaches flashpoint, get away from it for five minutes and calm down. Then find a quiet place to discuss the issue calmly. Try not to let them get to you – don't let them win!*

If all else fails, then ultimately you will have to formally discipline the compulsive difficult person. If they can't work with you, it is they who must go.

People principles

Learning the skills of how best to deal with people should be one of your highest priorities as a first-time manager.

Get on the right track to honing your people skills

1. Your team will not perform effectively unless all of its members understand fully their roles and the team's objectives. Spell it out clearly and reinforce your message continuously.

2. You will have to convince your people that you are committed, so be enthusiastic – it's contagious!

3. With a new team, seek out problems straight away and tackle them immediately. You may find they have suffered from poor management in the past, a distracting maverick character in their midst, or impossible working conditions. Set up an on-going appraisal system to get feedback and reverse the tide.

4. Don't assume that money is the only reason that people turn up for work. You can work on training your people, improving the climate at work and, even, bonding the team through activities outside the workplace.

5. Work on your leadership skills – show your staff that you are organised, well able to communicate and consistent in your expectations and they will be more inclined to respect you.

6. Don't get too hung up by the prospect of managing former colleagues or people older than yourself. On the whole, they will accept you as a manager if you treat them with respect and forthrightness. However, if you can foresee a challenge with certain individuals, don't ignore it. Get it out into the open.

7. If you experience the problem of managing difficult characters, attempt to find out if they have specific problems you can help them to overcome. Always remain as professional and composed as possible. However, remember that if their behaviour is so damaging that the team is severely handicapped you will have to use the full power of the company's disciplinary muscle. If somebody has to go, *they* have to go. Be ready for this situation.

In an economic sense, we are only worth the same as the value we add to the organisations to which we sell our time. If you can help people to move gently towards this realisation you are well on the way towards making the impact that will really get you noticed.

Chapter 4

DELIVERING TO THE BOTTOM LINE

What's in this chapter for you

Monitoring your own performance
Full-circle analysis
Appraising others
Get a quick overview from day one
What to do if you get stuck
Managing at a distance (homeworkers, reps etc.)
Working with numbers

> ❝ *I was feeling really pleased with how the first five months had gone. The team seemed well focused and happy and productivity seemed to be increasing. However, it transpired that we had been concentrating mainly on consolidating existing business and when three of our major customers went to the wall, we had a problem. I realise now that we should have taken time out to look impartially at what we were doing and developing a wider customer base.* ❞
> **– Steve Marshall, telesales manager**

As a manager, you will probably be at least one step removed from making the products or performing the services which make money for the organisation. However, the company has not added your managerial salary to its overheads just to impress the taxman. You will still be expected to generate value, so you must identify the areas in which you can do so. These should become your priorities in your new role.

What activities of managers can contribute hard value to the company? Think about your areas of responsibility – how could you increase their income-generating potential or reduce costs and improve efficiency?

Good managers add value by optimising the performance of themselves and their teams. The key to this is to have an appraisals mechanism which allows you constantly to review how you and your team are working and seek out ways to make improvements.

Monitoring your own performance

You will not expected to turn up on day one and be perfect at everything. You will experience a steep learning curve in your new job.

Nobody's perfect. Accept this statement categorically and without prejudice. We can all, however, be slightly better than we are now. Then we can be slightly better again. But how do you know what you need to do to move on and change?

> ❝ *I'd joined the company at a particularly difficult time, as we were consolidating our European subsidiaries and everything was absolutely frantic. My boss sent me a note through after a couple of weeks to say how pleased he was with my progress and how I'd got the team together. I hardly saw him over the next six months. I was then hauled into his office and told what a terrible job I was doing. I could not believe the transition and decided there and then to plan my escape route, which I did three months later.* ❞
> **– Peter Robinson, export director**

To begin with, you need to ensure that your perception of what constitutes a good job fits in with your boss's and that you all have the same priorities. As a new boss, you will need guidance and monitoring from your own line manager to ensure that you are pulling in the right direction.

Tips on staying in touch with your boss

❑ *Insist on regular consultations – don't barge into their office sit yourself down and start talking, but arrange regular half-hour sessions when specific issues can be thrashed out.*
❑ *Copy your boss in on all important correspondence – if something goes wrong, they cannot then turn round and say that you didn't keep them informed, and your successes will not be overlooked.*
❑ *Analyse your training and self-development needs and put forward a suggested and costed training programme for yourself and other members of your staff for discussion.*
❑ *Invite your boss to team meetings and ensure that he or she becomes involved in the discussions.*
❑ *Make sure that whatever appraisal systems are in place, your boss uses them effectively – see the next section for more on appraisals.*

Once you're clear about what you should be striving to achieve, it's time to put in place a means of assessing you own performance as measured against your own goals.

Full-circle analysis

One useful device for effective personal assessment is to undertake what's known as a 360-degree or full-circle analysis. This involves everybody with whom you work thinking about your efficacy. Your manager(s), your peers and your subordinates give a broad impression of your performance to date. This should reflect the critical success areas that define your job. The feedback from this is used as the basis for planning your personal development programme which in turn should help you to progress the ambitions of the organisation.

A note of warning, however. Do not undertake FCAs lightly. They should be properly structured (your HR people should have templates for undertaking them) and should apply to everyone in the organisation, not just yourself!

Appraising others

Traditionally, appraisals are seen in the same light as an annual visit to the dentist. They involve a hurried and embarrassed interview ("Do you think, Dilys, that your perfomance is good, satisfactory or unsatisfactory when using the photocopier?"), a flurry of form filling and a sigh of relief until next year.

Forget the ritual – appraisals are simply ways of helping people review how well they are doing and as such you need to ensure that you are appraising consistently and constantly.

> ❝ The current manager is great. I really look forward to our regular performance reviews. Everyone used to dread them. It felt like a police interrogation, spotlight in the face. Now they are more constructive. Our ideas are put first and foremost. It's really useful to know how well I'm doing and where I can improve. Nobody has ever taken this kind of interest in me before. ❞
> **– James Kegan, sales administrator**

Appraisal tips

❏ *Ensure that each member of the team knows what you expect them to be delivering – this then provides the benchmark against which their appraisal can take place.*
❏ *Keep notes on a daily basis as to what is going on in the department and refer to these constantly. By doing so you avoid the danger of assessing someone solely on a recent event (either excellent or catastrophic) which will distort your true impression.*
❏ *If trouble is brewing, resist the temptation to deal with it at the next appraisal. It may well be too late by then – tackle it head on, and now.*
❏ *Ensure that you fully understand the practicalities of the company's formal appraisal system. If you don't, get help. Nothing will undermine an appraisal more than if you are seen to be anything other than fully comfortable with it.*
❏ *Ensure that all face-to-face interviews are conducted in a relaxed and friendly atmosphere, that there are no interruptions and that you both feel comfortable. Don't tower over the interviewee and don't use harsh lights.*

Good appraisal skills are vital. The key is to remember that as a manager you should be appraising for 100 per cent of your time at work.

Get a quick overview from day one

To start up an effective appraisals process you will need to get a quick picture of the challenge you face. This will allow you to direct your efforts in the right way from day one.

It may be useful at the beginning to try to classify your staff within the following categories:

○ *Talent and seed corn for the future – these people will be anticipating what you need to be doing as part of your management agenda and could offer you the best source of help while you are finding your feet.*
○ *People who may be underperforming but could shift dramatically with the right support – they have just lost their focus and should be prime targets for your motivational efforts.*
○ *Misfits – fewer and fewer of these people survive but they present their managers with problems, not solutions, and you should be on high alert when dealing with them.*

What to do if you get stuck

You must be mature enough to admit that you may need help.
You are only human, after all, and cannot be expected to get
everything right first time.

> ❝ *I'd had real difficulty with the dispatch department,*
> *which was hopelessly understaffed. Rather than explaining the*
> *situation and involving all senior management to emphasise the*
> *urgency of getting the Middle East order out in 24 hours, I went*
> *straight in and shouted at them. The result was they downed tools*
> *and we nearly lost the business. I should have got*
> *help much earlier."*
> **– Janice Peterson, consignment manager**

Never see asking for help from either your staff or from your
boss as a sign of weakness. There is a lot of truth in the adage
"no man is an island".

In any situation where you have made a mistake, you need to
ensure that you do not dwell on it and let it eat you up. Be
positive and manage your way out of trouble with the help of your
team and your bosses. Remember: successful managers turn
mistakes into learning experiences.

Managing at a distance

How do you go about managing people that you don't see on a
daily basis? This problem applies to you if you are managing a
team of field sales reps, people who telecommute (a rapidly
growing phenomenon) or if you have responsibility for a satellite
branch of the business located a distance from your office,
perhaps overseas.

Your management efforts still need to be aimed at adding
value so you have to apply the same overall performance
appraisals as for your in-house staff and respond promptly to
satisfy their needs or iron out any problems.

How do you know your salesman is not reducing his golf handicap at your expense? What's to stop a homeworker watching television all day?

The fact is that managing at a distance does involve something of a leap of faith as, yes, trust can be abused. However, most jobs have measurable outcomes, things that you can quantify and monitor. With sales people performance is fairly easy to benchmark in terms of orders generated and new customers developed. Similarly with telecommuters, you should be able to quantify their efficiency against given norms and identify any possible problems when you see variations from what you expect.

Regular personal contact is vital. The trick here is to manage the fine balance between genuine interest and concern for their well-being and being seen to be spying on them.

Fortunately, new technology really does help here. E-mail and mobile phones give you ready access to your staff without being necessarily intrusive – phones can be switched off when with customers and the messaging system used; e-mails stored and retrieved when time allows.

Dealing with reps, homeworkers etc.

☐ *Ask for regular reports. Don't insist on too much detail or else report writing will become a full time job. Rather, design a form which will show you how much work has been undertaken and what has been achieved and ensure that this is sent in on a weekly basis.*
☐ *Commit to regularly visiting your distance workers and ensuring you set time aside to get to know them on informal basis. Arrange to have lunch or dinner with them. Similarly, with sales reps, spend time on the road with them visiting customers.*
☐ *Identify what people actually need in terms of support and advice, then deliver the support in a positive way.*

Avoid falling into the "out of sight, out of mind" trap. Just because you don't see them every day does not mean that they are any less important to you than anyone else.

Working with numbers

> ❝ *I'd come from a very low-tech, computer-phobic environment but I did know my way around a balance sheet or a profit and loss account. I knew my new company was fully computerised and I also realised that mastering the new equipment was an essential goal if I was to have a firm grasp of my team's financial performance. The first thing I did was to grab the best computer whiz in my department and get enough instant know-how to function in the first couple of days. I'm now booked on two courses which should put me fully in the picture.* ❞
> **– Dave Butler, sales manager**

A basic degree of numeracy is vital in today's management climate and usually this is the area which causes most new managers the greatest concern. You now may well be responsible for budgeting and forecasting. Even if you aren't, you still need to be able to look at the figures and understand them. How else can you estimate where you can add value to the organisation?

Ignore the financial side of your job at your peril. Delivering on the bottom line is a tangible goal and failure to do so will be deemed just that – failure. The excuse "I didn't understand" won't do.

We do not have the time in this book to give you a lesson in business finance. What we can do is give you some tips.

The keys to mastering the numbers game

❑ *Get involved in any financial planning or budgeting which is relevant to your department. Never hand over responsibility to others for it as this can result in underfunding or*

*overbudgeting, both of which could prove disastrous for
your career as a manager.*

❑ *Keep your team informed of all the financial implications of
their roles. Explain the terminology – even more incentive
for understanding it fully yourself!*

❑ *Commit to getting to grips with the numbers if you are weak
in this area. Go on appropriate courses, read the right
books, get the right software, ask the right people –
whatever it takes, just do it!*

How to add value

Remember that, as a manager, you will be expected to make a
financial contribution to the company through your actions.

Concentrate your efforts on performance management

1. In a new managerial role, one of your most pressing
   tasks should be to identify where your team or
   department can make an impact on the financial health
   of the company. Look for areas where you could
   potentially make savings or a larger contribution.

2. Make it clear to every member of your staff how and
   where their actions affect the company's bottom line
   and vigorously encourage an appreciation of these facts.

3. A key tool which will help your value-adding aspirations
   is an effective appraisal process. This goes beyond the
   ritualised annual formal interview and form-filling
   exercise prevalent in many companies – you should
   appraise your staff 100 per cent of the time you are at
   work, using the notes you make along the way to sum
   things up in the formal appraisal.

4. Don't forget to appraise your own performance. You
   could try full-circle analysis, in which your subordinates,
   peers and managers give feedback on how you're doing.

5. Never be afraid to seek help either from your team or
   your bosses. If you are having difficulties, use the
   experience positively as a learning tool and ask for
   advice from every source available to you.

6.   If you are faced with a team which is not office-based, make time for regular meetings with them and establish mutually agreeable performance benchmarks which are checked regularly.

7.   When measuring performance in terms of your team's contribution to company value you must be competent with figurework. If you are not confident in your numeracy skills or your ability to use a system you are unfamiliar with, find help from within the company immediately so you can at least make a start and then book yourself on to courses to hone your skills. Improving your own ability is part of increasing the team's potential for generating a positive and demonstrable financial impact on the bottom line.

Others will admire your management prowess if you have a good handle on performance management. And, the more people-focused you can make this, the better.

What's in this chapter for you

Doing and delegating
What to delegate
Planning training
Personal development for you and your team
The Brilliant Manager's golden rules

We have seen so far in this book the techniques and skills you can use as you start your management career. This last chapter will look towards the future at how you grow and develop yourself and your team.

Doing and delegating

As a new manager, it's likely you will be eager to roll up your sleeves and throw yourself fully into your job. Keen to make an impression both on your staff and on your boss, you will wish to be as helpful and hard working as possible.

> **❝** *It seems to me that my predecessor had done very little but sit in her office writing reports and bossing people around. I considered myself to be more hands-on and consequently I got much more involved. Any work that got passed down from my boss I'd undertake without hesitation. If the phone rang, I'd answer it and deal with any queries myself. I even told my team that if they had too much on I'd help! The result was that several of the slacker members dumped projects on me – I ended up unable to cope and totally stressed out.* **❞**
> **– Wendy Spencer, customer service manager**

Wendy's problem is very common. She wanted to be seen to be effective and supportive, but ended up snowed under. She considered that to ask for help would be seen as a weakness in everybody's eyes and so took on more and more work. Quite simply, she failed to recognise the importance of delegating.

To avoid the same problems Wendy had, you need to be able to recognise the danger signals.

> **Are any of these situations familiar?**
>
> ❑ *Staff come to you repeatedly with petty problems that they should be able to sort out for themselves.*
> ❑ *You spend an inordinate amount of time checking and double-checking other people's work.*
> ❑ *You consider it the norm to take work home with you.*
> ❑ *You are first in to work and the last to leave.*
> ❑ *You are reluctant to pass work to others because you don't think it would be done as well as if you did it yourself.*

You must appreciate that delegation is an essential management tool. You need to become confident in yourself and your staff in order to empower those around you. Without it your team will never work effectively.

Be aware of and avoid getting locked into the following mindsets when developing your delegation skills:

○ *"What happens if they make a mistake? I'll get the blame for not doing it in the first place."*
○ *"What's the point of my being here if I'm not getting involved?"*
○ *"My predecessor always found time for this task – it will look as if I can't cope if I change now."*
○ *"I'm getting the management salary so I should be doing the job."*

What to delegate

❝ *When I finally realised delegation was the key to sorting out my problems, I spent the next six months gradually finding the right people for the right tasks. I have learnt that to delegate properly takes time and continual refinement. I feel I am much better at it now and it's taken a great deal of pressure off me.* ❞
– Wendy Spencer

You need to work out very quickly a strategy for dividing up your work. Start with the mundane tasks, like opening the post, filing, picking up the answerphone messages or answering incoming calls. A huge amount of expensive management time can be wasted doing these sorts of task.

Think of the truly routine activities which you find yourself doing in the first few weeks as a manager. List them. Now look at the staff in your team and write down against each item the name of somebody in the department who could have done that task.

To begin with, concentrate on the smaller tasks which are eating your time and stopping you from doing what you're paid to do. As you gain in experience and your knowledge of your staff increases, you will learn to delegate more important tasks as a way of keeping your team challenged.

Tips for effective delegation

- Allocate tasks to members of your team in accordance with their strengths.
- Present the tasks you are delegating as a challenge and a means of showing trust.
- Always offer support and training when asking someone to take on a new task.
- Always discuss the tasks you are delegating face to face with those involved and never decide to delegate without fully consulting with them.
- Make it clear to your staff how frequently you expect to be consulted about the work you have delegated.
- Let go! Once you have delegated, offer support and help if necessary, but don't interfere.
- Don't be tempted to pass over just the boring work. This might free your time but it will also demotivate your staff.

Delegation takes time to develop but it is a skill you have to master in order to succeed as a manager. Not only will it make you more efficient but it will also help you to recognise the talents and needs of those around you. By doing so, you will have a solid foundation on which to plan for your own and your staff's future success.

Planning training

When considering your own and your team's training needs you need to consider the big picture.

> What are your true aspirations? Think also about the aspirations of your staff. How can you achieve these goals for yourself and them?

Your plans for the future should include a training needs analysis. This will look at both formal and informal learning needs. Some of these may be satisfied by course-based training – like business law or accountancy etc. – which leads to a formal qualification at the end. This requires a large commitment of time and money over a long period.

Other forms of training are less formal and are based on expanding awareness. These might include such things as assertiveness training, or public speaking.

The world is changing at a dramatic rate and you need to insure against both your own and your team's obsolescence.

> Look at your company's annual report and mission statements. Where are they going to be in the next two years? The next five years? Do you and your team have the necessary skills to be there too? Identify your training needs from this kind of document and it should enable you to be linked automatically to the needs of the business.

Try to take a long-term view of the skills and needs of yourself and your department.

> For you and your team, analyse the following:
>
> ❑ *Skills and competencies*
> ❑ *Personal strengths and weaknesses*
> ❑ *Interpersonal skills*
> ❑ *Ambitions.*

Much of this information can be gathered from the continuous appraisals that you should be committed to and from your own boss's appraisal of you.

You can quickly pick up on the needs of your team. If a certain member is poor with customers on the phone then the obvious answer is to get them some telephone technique training. Similarly if you find addressing big groups of people a daunting scenario, then a public speaking course with video technology would be ideal.

> ❝ *The company I joined paid lip service to training needs but allocated a pitifully inadequate budget to it. I bounded in, full of energy, analysed my team who had never received formal training and at the end of the first month presented a proposed training budget to my boss. He looked at me as if I was mad and in no uncertain terms told me that there was no money allocated for training that year. I felt completely thwarted.* ❞
> **– Steve Cross, area manager**

So what do you do if, as is likely, you come in when all the training budgets have been decided for the year and you recognise key areas that need to be tackled immediately?

Work out how to get your own way

- ❏ *Find out immediately how budgets are allocated for next year and stake your claim – now! Lobby hard. Circulate appropriate reports quantifying the costs involved but showing the benefits in financial terms to the business.*
- ❏ *Is there anyone in personnel responsible for in-house training? If so, can you persuade them to informally, and at no cost to your department, hold some relevant session to cover some of your immediate problems?*
- ❏ *The chances are, everyone in the team will excel at something. Organise informal sessions on particular themes and get the best people to explain how they succeed and what their mental approach is. They may be nervous to do this in front of their peers so you should ensure that you facilitate the process. If you get these activities right, they work extremely well and build great team morale.*
- ❏ *Are there relevant training videos available (or even, dare we say it, books!) the costs of which can be creatively "hidden"? Hiring training videos for the day or buying books is not a major outlay and it is possible you could cover the costs (mistakenly, of course!) out of your own expenses or petty cash.*

Personal development for you and your team

A theme running through this book is that success for you and for your team starts and ends with you. You determine all the parameters.

Who you are as a person has an obvious bearing upon how effectively you adapt to the management role. If you don't feel right about yourself then managing others well will prove to be very difficult indeed.

Accurate self-analysis is a process which you should try to undertake on a regular basis and you should encourage this in your team. It can be incredibly difficult and sometimes painful – but really effective people will undertake it all of the time.

Look at the needs of yourself and the team now and in the future. How many of the following statements apply?

- ❑ *The standard response to changing a system is "Why – we've always done it like that."*
- ❑ *You need to be more creative.*
- ❑ *Most people feel that they lack long-term job security.*
- ❑ *If asked to take on a new role, the immediate response will be "I can't".*

You need to look closely at the mental baggage people are carrying which is stopping them from growing and developing. So, always present any change as an exciting development, a way to avoid boredom, or a challenge. Assure them of adequate training. If a lack of creativity is the problem, use brainstorming sessions, role play or management games to get people to expand their minds and look for new solutions. If it is a question of security, it would be duplicitous of you to claim that all of you have jobs for life – the world is no longer like that. However, you can present the environment they are in as a fun place to be and uncertainty as a challenge and a counterbalance to boredom.

The concept of the "learning organisation" where everyone fits into a positive success culture has been identified as providing employees with necessary support to be more open and to take more risks. If possible, encourage the team to work to change themselves. This is where personal development comes into play.

You have learnt so far how to analyse yourself and your team in terms of current needs. Thus if a new software package is introduced, the people using it will need to learn all about it. This is satisfying a current operational need. Personal development, however, tries to recognise future needs.

> " *Gill was great in the sales office. She was totally on top of the admin, brilliant on the phone and was very popular with all of the team. At her appraisal we discussed where she would go next and she said she wanted to go out on the road as a sales negotiator. I saw her potential too, but the trouble with her, and she agreed here, was that she was easily manipulated and walked over. We decided the best course of action was to get her on an assertiveness course and then put her on the road. It worked – she's excellent!* "
> **– Pauline Barnes, estate agent**

Pauline had identified a future role for a team member and ensured that the training and support was given to enable her to progress, both professionally and emotionally.

Why should you bother trying to predict the future in this way? Quite simply, if you don't, you will have a stagnant and, ultimately, bored team. Personal development is about:

○ *Getting people to feel better about themselves*
○ *Building up loyalty – it shows you have their own best interests at heart*
○ *Increasing their capacity to take more on by enhancing their skill base*
○ *Keeping them interested and happy.*

By getting it right, you will have a settled and challenged team not of dull "lifers" but of people who are genuinely interested and challenged by what is going on around them.

The Brilliant Manager's golden rules

By now, you should be looking forward to your future success as a manager. You've learnt about people skills and you've seen the importance of planning for the future. All of these skills will need to be refined and developed over time, but they are the key to being a successful manager.

This last part of the book offers you some core advice on the issues which you will face in your first management position. Take whatever you can from it – many of the points are covered more fully in other books in the *60 Minutes Success Skills Series*, each being too lengthy to attempt to cover here.

These are the qualities of a brilliant manager

1. Recognise stress! It often encroaches on all aspects of life, particularly the link between work and home. Stress distorts perceptions and means that everything appears to be overwhelming. Often the pressures can build up almost imperceptibly. Make sure you maintain your interests outside of work and that your professional life does not dominate your personal life.

2. Learn how to listen! Listening is every bit as important a skill as talking yet few people recognise the fact. In the crucial process of continuously appraising and developing your team, truly two-way communication is vital.

3. Master time – don't be a slave to it! Time management will be crucial to your success and you need to master it quickly. Analyse early on how you are spending your time and work on eradicating those things (and people!) which are keeping you from being constructive.

4. Get organised! Untidiness in the office will not only make you inefficient but also make you look as though you couldn't care less. Get on top of the paperwork quickly – find out if it's necessary, and recruit help from your team.

5. Leave work at work! Don't take work home as a matter of course. Sometimes it will be essential but, as a rule, avoid it. You should be able to fit everything into a normal working day – by taking work home you will simply make yourself tired and you'll be increasingly likely to suffer from stress.

6. Delegate! A crucial skill to develop is the art of delegation. Identify what tasks you could delegate and then find the right person for each of them. Consult fully

with those to whom you intend to pass the work and offer support. Start with small tasks and hand over interesting work as well as the chores.

7. If in doubt, ask! You will not be expected to know everything. There is nothing wrong with asking for help and advice from those around you – that's what successful teams are all about – and it's certainly better than making a mistake because you were afraid to.

8. Say thank you! No matter how busy you are, good manners count for a lot and people are motivated when their hard work is recognised and appreciated.

9. Never stop planning! If you are not constantly thinking ahead, both for yourself and your staff, then you will stagnate and become obsolete. Look to the future and the challenges it holds with confidence.

10. Learn from mistakes! Mistakes happen – recognise this fact. When you do something wrong, be honest and encourage others to do likewise. Learn from the error and find ways to ensure the same problem can't arise again.

11. Be true to yourself! You need to be natural, both as a manager and as a manager. People will find it impossible to respect you if you are play acting.

If you follow these basic rules, and all the other tips and techniques given throughout this book, you will find your first management role rewarding and exciting. You will also be on your way to a successful career as a manager.